Natural
Defenses

Susan Terris

Marsh Hawk Press New York 2004

Natural Defenses

MARSH HAWK PRESS

ISBN 0-9724785-5-8

Library of Congress Cataloging-in-Publication Data

Terris, Susan.
  Natural defenses / Susan Terris.– 1st ed.
     p. cm.
  ISBN 0-9724785-5-8
  I. Title.
  PS3570.E6937N37 2003
  811'.54–dc22

                                        2003015906

First Edition

Book design by Jeremy Thornton
Cover: Henri Rousseau, "Fight Between a Tiger and a Buffalo," 1908 (detail),
        reproduced with permission of the Cleveland Museum of Art.
        A gift of the Hanna Fund, 1949.
Author photograph by Margaretta K. Mitchell
Background photograph by Jeremy Thornton

Marsh Hawk Press
P.O. Box 220, Stuyvesant Station
New York, NY 10009
http://www.marshhawkpress.org

For Myra, a woman of valor...

Acknowledgments

"Death Notes in C Minor," *American Literary Review*

"Color Of Tomorrow," "Who Can Convince the Sea to be Reasonable?" Blue Unicorn

"The Night Mind," *The Cape Rock*

"Monday Is an Abstract Concept," "And What Was That Beating in the Night? / Were They Planets or Horseshoes?" *The Comstock Review*

"What Is the Distance in Round Meters / Between the Sun and the Oranges?" The Comstock Review

"Gorëme," *Connecticut Review*

"You Don't Believe That Dromedaries / Keep Moonlight in their Humps?" *Dogwood*

"What Has Been Lost, " "Singita: Artful Matter," *The Drunken Boat*

"Pantoum for a Member of the Wedding," *Flyway, PoetryMagazine.com*

"At The Bone," *Flyway*

"Day at Caunos," *Full Circle, A Journal of Poetry and Prose.*

"Natural Defenses," *Haight Ashbury Literary Review, OnThePage*

"Butterfly Dreams," *Jewish Women's Literary Annual*

"Fugue State," *The Kansas Quarterly/Arkansas Review*

"Boxcar At The Holocaust Museum," *Many Mountains Moving, Noe Valley Voice*

"Rough And Unsugared," "The Iron Handle Of Innisfree," *The Missouri Review*

"Rough And Unsugared," *Passages North*

"Shadow Of A Falling Bird," "Lie Of The Ordinary Life," *Ploughshares, PoetryMagazine.com*

"Blind-Fish Cave," *Poet Lore*

"The Iron Handle Of Innisfree," *PoetryMagazine.com*

"Dark Matter," *Pudding Magazine*

"In The Familiar Tense," *A Room Of One's Own, Whiskey Island*

"Afterimages," *Salt Hill*

"Deathscapes," *SF Bay Guardian, The Sun, ZuZu's Petals Online*

"Flight To Primitive Passions," "Violet, The Earthquake Girl," *Spillway*

"Ice Maiden," "Lucid Dreaming," *The Spoon River Poetry Review*

"Night-Tigers," *Tiger's Eye*

"Hidden Child," *Tikkun*

"The Woman On Death Row Watches TV," *UAS Explorations, Clackamas Literary Review*

"Undercut," *Wind*

"Wakeful Rest," *ZeBookZine*

Some of the poems in this book have been published in **EYE OF THE HOLOCAUST**, published in 1999 by Arctos Press.

Some of the poems in this book have been published in **KILLING IN THE COMFORT ZONE** and in **SUSAN TERRIS: GREATEST HITS**, chapbooks published in 1995 & 2000 by Pudding House Publications.

"Dark Matter" was published in **GLASS WORKS**, Pudding House Publications, 2003

"Lunar Plexus" was published as "Self-Portrait in Wool" in **SO LUMINOUS THE WILDFLOWERS**, Tebot Bach, 2003.

The following poems have been printed as broadsides:
"Afterimages", *The Muse Press;* Carmel, CA
"Natural Defenses", *The Center for Book Arts;* New York, NY
"At the Bone", *San Francisco Center for Book Arts*

Table of Contents

Natural Defenses

Afterimages

What Has Been Lost:

Star-wishes, the courage to step on a crack.

How to speak with innocence,
wait at someone's feet, follow deer through brush.
To apologize and mean it.

Baby teeth in the silk pouch,
the man who wrote his own obituary,
Father and his father, the delicate touch of a fingertip,
the diamond pin, the right breast.

Map to the territory of the unlived life.

Art of paddling whitewater or staunching blood.
How to guide a marionette, rub sticks for fire.
How to make one kiss matter.

The range of freedom. What the golden eagle might tell
about pursuit and betrayal.

The day foxes come from their dens
and salamanders from under their rocks.

Dream of rising from bed to fly alone through night cirrus,
greedy and heedless.

The fugitive pieces to the puzzle of the self.

The sexual jolt of the earthquake and its aftershocks.
How to decode other voices of the wild
whispering from marsh and river and sea.

All this relinquished, bargaining, bargaining,
bargaining again for ease instead of edge.

Lucid Dreaming

She sees herself as a traveler
with the world in motion and scenery
shifting, so she can't look back
and wonder who it was she used to be.

Shadowed, she knows the taste of longing:
honey on the lips, salt on the tongue.
Its texture—lambswool
uncarded yet soft.
Its sound—a song of yesterday,
blue echo on the morning;
but the scent of change is in the air
and she follows it.

Since longing seems weightless,
she's sure she can pull threads of
the dream, spin them
to mark her path. What she does,
her shadow repeats.
She shuttles in and out. It does, also.
She stops, starts. Her shadow follows.
At last, fingertips joined,

the two uncoil strands, begin to rappel
into the dark warp of a well
where they are safe, where
daylight stars can blink and beckon.

The Lie Of The Ordinary Life

A muster of white peacocks preens
by the inverted lake pooling the ceiling.
The peacocks are mute.

He is not quite mute. An inattention.
Letters answered in such haste, he fails
to answer. Words overlaid,
commas sliding out of line—a riff
of lost eyelashes punctuating nothing.

In this hungry place, there is a bed and a sign
noting the danger of temporary tattoos.

"I think," he tells her when they've fed one another
raspberries and champagne grapes,
"you may find me too ordinary."

An ivory plume breezes down, not yet knifed
into pen or dipped into black-squid ink.

His gift to her: a silver arrow lancing
an amber heart. And, of course,
the dense sweetness of his soap, his skin
on the pewter of her silky burn-out gown.
Her gift to him: a magic stone left behind.

Then the peacocks screech.
Gravity arrested, the plume begins to fall up
toward the mirage. Lake. Sky. A void.

In The Familiar Tense

When Mary's Belgian griffon died, Degas wrote friends,
begging them to find, at any price, a new one

    Mary Cassatt. When she and Edgar Degas met,
    she was thirty-three. Autumn, Paris....

and send it to Paris parcel post. *She wants a young dog,*
a very young one that will love her.

    Degas loved her. Forty years of closeness,
    yet both too restrained

Careful not to nudge his elbow with hers, Mary
held the new pup in her arms and leaned forward

    for sex without marriage.
    A marriage, instead, of minds:

so he could feel the heat from her breath.
That autumn we met, she murmured, *then* —

    as he proposed her for
    the 4th Impressionist Exhibition,

Don´t, he cautioned. *I´m just an old man who likes horses*
as you like dogs....

and she brought him to American collectors,
gave him her money, her touch.

Stroking the dog's muzzle, Mary let its silken warmth
soothe her. *When we met, then I began to live.*

And when he lost his will to live,
she found a niece to care for him.

Degas leaned back in the bentwood chair. Closed his eyes.
Tais toi, he said. *Be still.*

Lunar Plexus

From the lunar plexus I arose like a hungry trout
and was caught fast on the sharp barbed hook
that hangs inside all once–beautiful–faces.

                                    Leonora Carrington

In magnetic air, my self or shadows of it,
the body a ballast for the head,
as I, smiling mask dragging an afghan body,
knit a new face from cosmic wool.

A three-dimensional life is formed by attitude.

You want what I have, so I must sheer
invisible sheep, comb and card
the fleece, twist the thread, ply needles,
then teach you how to do the same.

All done with mist and a mirror or two.

Still, don´t expect to touch flesh. This wool
is thin, porous, soft but without affect
and, its anxious thread tugged by
an unseen hook, keeps on unraveling.

At The Bone

Perverse, he said. *You're not brave. Just perverse,*
he repeated when she said she liked snakes.

The grass parts, a shadow weaves. Cool to the
touch. Dry. Once as a girl, on a hot-sun morning,
she caught one, taught him calm. Lidless eyes were
trusting as he smelled her with his y-shaped tongue.
In someone else's hands: gyration and panic,
yet in hers again: calm. After a day,
she left him by the turkey feather fungus
on the birch stump where she'd found him.

But he wasn't her only snake. Others, stand-ins
for the one from Eden that whispered of
knowledge, appeared. A choice between innocence
and depth, an election of layered views.
Snake and sin: an apple-cheeked complexity.
The unknown. She always chose it. Punishment
and pain before ignorance.
Not the poet's *zero at the bone,* but the sinousness

of spine, miracle of shedding skin, curious tongue.
Mouth open, silently alert. A darkness alive.

Natural Defenses

A risk-taker, I've never mastered
the art of protection

as a tree defends itself
against a giraffe
with bitter tannin that stops forage
and warns downwind
of danger. Or as a trout
hooked in a river
releases pheromones to alert
those swimming downstream.

Your reflexes, the fisherman warned,
slow down as you get older.

He was not speaking of fishing,
of course. But I,
disarmed by a taste for intensity,
less savvy than
trout or tree, forgot
to prepare myself for pain.
Even an old giraffe
remembers to browse upwind.

Night-Tigers

How had he come to her in the night? she wondered.
Breath warm. Tiger breath. She'd been dreaming
of tigers, sprinting with them through jungles
flush with tropical blossoms.

It's safe, he insisted, taking hold of her and angling
his body next to hers. But the tigers, whiskers
twitched and paws splayed in mud, were stalking.
Inhaling their pheromones, she followed
the darkness behind their ears and at the tips
of their tails

and abandoned the country of men. Hands fell
away. Flesh, too. And she had no words. Her words
had been swallowed by the tigers
as they licked her lips with their tongues,
ran them and their claws along her thighs.
She heard them chuffing, was aware she should be
staring them down, but instead she
pulled away and fled

into the broadleaf foliage
dragging a striped shawl stained with blood.
Then she ran and ran—seeking not safety
but deeper, darker coverage.

Afterimages

Paint a picture with afterimages only with all the first colors gone — only afterimages —and carry it so you have some 3rd and 4th afterimages. Study the aftercolors of any and all objects and only paint the aftercolor.

–Ivan Albright

Doorbell, door, corridor, rain-studded coat, face smooth, ears rough, neck arching, cheek-on-cheek, mouths, the weight of morning, heat and smoke, tiger-time, clothes twisted, quilt and spread twisted, mango ripe, music, coffee—first the image, then luster and refraction

and with the prime pigment gone, repaint, feel brush beneath ribs again and again until *doorbell coat-damp* bristles lose thrust, until a not-something is a scrim of something *knob twisted parquet patchwork quilt* that happened then *Puccini* and again and again to a person *rumpled shirt empty cup corridor mouth ripe* who may have been you

like in the quilted field of Tuscan flowers: wine and song, ruby figs, snake grass and wild oats now sepiaed with time *mango skin buttercup bed-spread bottleneck tongue and groove* from bright emerald to moss to celadon to patina *claret to peach to blush to milk to water* muscle sleeked to bone *cheek-heat out-of-doors wild snake rough-smoke* as color tints *parquet of morning* bleed into a faint patchwork a negative grace, image over image, multiplicity *viola nude descending lip-music ripe oak and tannen bent tiger bells* light-streaks through prisms *rain-smoke* landscape of then and now *morning-weight arch after-taste* subtlety of nuance *damp-twisted grass aria* and the afterimage of afterimage of afterimage *hair-spreading quilt-rumple door coffee spill* eye-echoes known *sheet-music* yet never again felt *coda* as story becomes vignette becomes moment becoming pause and

       hands morning door to corridor ears patched breath cheeks coffee to buff green to ripe face-saving fig-flesh oat-spilling light—bright to dim then dimmer *rain-stripes* so shade *snake-smooth* scent so scumble and see it thin *butterfly tongue* and *mango-poppy arch of smoke* until afterimages all merge *singers* the center pales *wing-shiver rain heat-spread lips brushing* then aftercolor washes at margins *the singing* objects *door the wild song* objectivity *the verse* rods and color-wands *the line bell the vibrato* straw and shadow matter *the rough silence*

Butterfly Dreams

The sky is bright with butterfly wings.
They fan from eucalyptus—stained-glass
radiant overhead. From one year
to the next, five generations live and die,
yet they return. Though the old woman
watches, she's ready to give up
monarchs with everything else.

Chuang-tzu, the ancient philosopher,
once dreamed he was a butterfly
breezing in sunlight; yet when he woke,
he was unsure if he was a man
who'd dreamed he was a butterfly.
Or a butterfly who'd dreamed he was a man.

Once, I had a dress like that, the old woman
whispers, as thousands of butterflies gild
the air. *Silky and thin. Once I waltzed
on satin feet that never touched ground.
So, come close, and hold me. Yes, like that.
Yes....*

Chuang-tzu and the old woman are dancing
in the glade. They move in a cloud
of yellow-orange. She tries to tell him
of the butterfly dress. He wants to tell her
the monarch has a claw at the bottom of
its frail leg. But leaves of blue-green eucalyptus
rattle, and all is lost in the January wind.

Undercut

We're holding hands, breathing hard.
The overhang, a limestone cliff,
part of a mountain, should last forever,
yet as we pause here—rock can't
withstand the persistence of water—
the creek is claiming it.

Basins are rounded by it, polished
until we shield our eyes in sunlight.
The glacial-tinted falls
slowly scours a wider hole.
Above us, fever of red-orange lichen
and firs awed by silvered moss.

Below, the canyon's deepest cut,
once limestone, now only space.
Each year the creek-song grows fainter.
While we stand gazing down, rock is
disappearing. Nothing is static.
Not lichen, not fir, not water, not breath.

The Color Of Tomorrow

Only through time time is conquered.
Burnt Norton, T.S. Eliot

Chagall´s lovers kiss in space. A blue cow nibbles sky.
Flowers burgeon in darkness beneath the earth,
and ocean depths teem with foam-flecked horses.
It´s January and plum trees blush
as the last persimmons rust on knobbed branches.

Yesterday´s shadows are sweet on the tongue,
but how do we sample today? Can we drink the wind?
What happens if we wrap time in our arms
and try to inhale its wildness? Does a fruitful year
weigh more or less than a barren one?

Sometimes words are echoes of night-rain
and we sip their mystery, but sometimes they mantle
skies like aurora borealis filling us with sheen
of the north and heat of the south. Is an hour
a decent portion? Can hunger be measured in days?

Like Chagall´s lovers we kneel in cloud to drink
from the teats of the blue cow. How rich are
milk-tailed comets? What color is tomorrow
and how will it taste? we ask floating into canyons
of a thousand sunsets or welcoming the chrysalis

of dawn. Yes, you are beside me, but I am alone
stretching to measure the distance to darkness.
I change direction once, then again. I am still
hungry. How good is a promise? Have I dared enough?
Is that your hand holding mine? How long is now?

Fugue State

Violet, The Earthquake Girl

Pale and blue-white as her handsewn chemise,
she's wandered 90 years
amid urns in the Columbarium.
At night, the watchman glimpses thin arms and legs,
smells her unwashed hair, hears the rales
of her giddy child's breath.

She moves, he insists, in careless bursts of color,
veering from dark into light and back
again as she searches. When the walls
peel away, she walks through a forest
sweeping leaves with a twig broom.
As the path clears, she follows it,
sucking on damask plums
shaken from trees overhead. Her hands

are transparent in starlight,
feet, too, as she prowls, searching for
her home, for mother, father, brother, sister—
lost with the doorways, windows, china,
and mirrors and the 7 times 7 times 7
of broken, untended dreams.

Little Red Rose, 1938

O little red rose!
Humankind lies in greatest need!
Humankind lies in greatest pain!
  Urlicht (Primal Light) –Gustav Mahler

As she twisted her jumping rope
at her waist so she could dance
Herr Krieger's dog, a man
with a stick crossed the street.

Soon Papa will come, she told him,
aware of her smooth plaits,
of her new red dress,
and we'll have sugar bread.

Jew, he said, hooking her rope with
the end of his stick. *Dirty Jew.*

Oh, no, the child answered,
it's my birthday,
and I've just had a bath.
Then with a curtsey she turned

from the man, put the front paws
of Herr Krieger's dog
on her shoulders and began
to teach it how to waltz.

The Hidden Child

I was good. We were all good Dutch children—
those of us who survived.

Before the Nazis, *Moeder* brandished other
threats—potatoes that would grow behind
unwashed ears, rats that might nest in
unkempt hair. Then jackboots on cobblestone
began to punctuate days and nights.
In our attic room, no soccer balls
or bicycles, no tulips; and sometimes
we ate dog meat to survive.

My daughter asks about the taste.
I say I don't remember. She probes what's
meant by good: *How good is good,* she
wonders, keen to quantify. Imagining me
studious, parsing days for later profit,
she cannot fathom the card games, flatness,
waste. She says I'm hooded,
use time as a weapon. It is. It was...

One time, when meat was scarce,
those who concealed us rode their bikes
past Sunday soccer to dig up tulip bulbs.
We roasted them, peeled the brown,
and ate them. *As I chewed,*
I thought *tulip, tulip* and tried to let
the flower I could not see
bloom inside.

Last year when the hidden ones met, I did not go.
I told my daughter I was out of time.

Boxcar At The Holocaust Museum

Assaulted by brick and steel, my sister and I cross
the glass bridge between then and now, touch
Szumsk, the Polish town
our grandparents came from, walk into
Ejszyszki Tower eyeing photo doppelgängers
of relatives we call the monkey aunts,
of an uncle who couldn't skate the '36 Olympics,
of our parents, ourselves.

My younger sister has married a Baptist, raised
children who don't believe they are Jews;
yet she—riveted—is moving snail's-pace.
So when I come upon it, I am alone.
It's an old red cattle car like those from
our Missouri childhood, counted as they
clacked by full of livestock
due for slaughter. But this one is different.
To avoid passing through, I pretend to examine
oxidized razors, forks, tea strainers, then metal
instruments of torture which up-close
become umbrella frames. I check my watch,
consider flight...

yet as I turn, I see my sister
by the boxcar unwilling to enter. *Why are
we here?* Hurrying toward her, I move past
cart, suitcases, hat boxes. *What will it tell us?*
For a moment, we are side by side, aware of
primal, physical comfort. Then together we step in.
It is dark. We do not speak. After 50 years,
stench still saturates the boards. As I inhale it,
I feel fingers tug at my pleated skirt,
at my sweater, my hands. Sweaty heads
I can't see butt me, begging for refuge,
those who would not have been spared:
my children, my sister's Mischling children,
my own Mischling grandchildren.

Suddenly, a soprano voice echoes around us.
Choo-choo. Turning, we see a boy-child
havened between parents.
He smiles, nods sweetly, beckoning to us and to
the invisible hordes pressed close. *Choo-choo,*
he repeats. *Choo-choo. All aboard....*

Fugue State

She is in a fugue state. There are holes
in her arm made by the fat man with suitcase
and Uzzi.
As her husband, a red blossom spreading across
his chest, lies in her lap, she hears screams
and mewling. A swift—if imperfect—shield,
he'd wedged his body in front of hers.
Now while she cries, odd sounds
chirr from his throat.
She feels burning, numbness; and when she looks up,
tinted windows of his office
pewter the sky.
Somehow, he'd punched an outside line
so she could plead for help.
Now, though time creeps, they wait.
I'm dying, he manages, as cones from spotlights
sear, *and we need to say good-bye.*

This is only shock, she tells herself. Help
will come. Things will be all right.
We'll have children and beachcomb in Kauai.

Week-old tulips, ones she'd bought
for his birthday, gape in the crystal bowl
atop the desk. They are scarlet,

yet not as scarlet as the bouquet mantling his shirt.
Nothing again will ever be real, she murmurs.
I am beyond the rainbow.
Today is yesterday inside out. Tomorrow
is upside down. I was young, and now I am old,
because there are holes in him. In me, too:
both of us are leaking.
If there were holes in time, I would inch
backwards with him, babe in my arms,
seal them over, lullaby us into yesterday.
Or I would tell him how the wizard told the sultan
the earth is held up on the back of
a giant elephant, and the elephant stands on
the back of a giant turtle. After that,
of course, it´s turtles—turtles, all the way down....

For them, the past was always overture. But now
his parched lips snap, turtle-like yet mute;
and past is everything, for she is in a fugue state.

The Woman On Death Row Watches TV

Live wires arc and burn in snow. Branches are iced.
They snap and shatter into devil's fingers. This spring,
willow trees, their limbs sheared, will have no leaves.
She sees herself, too, on TV, her face spliced
with cracked trees falling on cars. People are frosted
to the bone. Feet numb yet they struggle to endure.
But others will die. They have
no water, no heat, no light. She prays for them.

Cold through the veins, they say, is the first
a person feels. A snake inching toward the heart.
An ice that burns. Then twitches, jerks, a cough,
silence, a doctor with a stethoscope.
And this will happen, this injection,
because she was a girl, wild with drugs, who wielded
an axe. But, in prison, she unthawed, tried on
beauty and God. Too late, she became someone else.

In the TV glacier, bones of boar and mammoth
in a slow-moving river that compresses
ice to dense, uncanny marble. Other bones, those of a girl
a thousand years old, lie with them, skin leathered,
body and limbs shrouded and fetus
cocooned in her belly. She'd been godless, immune
to rules, someone who'd killed, cast in alive.
And, in a blue crevasse, she'd clawed against oblivion.

Hypothermia. Not from a glacier but a plunge into
chilled water like she saw in the trailer for Titanic.
Needles of pain and delerium. Burning below
in a too-cold cave, its air sucked by fire. This is a pagan
hell. Styx is a river of ice. On TV, Charon
steers a boat but, here, a sled, and she's sheened with ice.
In a whiteout, she killed someone. More than one.
Now she burns and freezes. Life is here. No, it is not.

Nor is God. Willows will have no leaves but fingers
of ice. No heat. No light. And they will die.

Shadow Of A Falling Bird

The shadow of a falling bird against a building
is more real than the bird.
Shadow of a glioblastoma on an MRI
is not real at all.

It may be short and brutal, the doctor says.

She sees the shadow of her own profile
on his shirt, sees a framed photo of
the shadow of a bi-plane across foothills
in the Valley of the Queens.

An approximation of truth,
only one measure of reality. She hears
the doctor's voice in the hard sanity
of morning, in the gray uncertainty of morning.

Monday Is An Abstract Concept

Dog days of summer: Sirius rises at sunset, sets at dawn.
Old news, but her brain is unable to track present tense.
The glio is growing again, forcing paperchains
of days to unlink. Now she sits for hours in the meadow
where Willa Cather wrote, watching honeybees,
listening to the *chuk-chuk* of chipmunks and brush
of redwings. Since she's lost numbers,
one to one-hundred scallop the air in random order
along with the black-white-gold predator above
who chills her with his nameless shadow.

August, no longer the eighth month, has become
an old college friend. She and August speak of God
and white magnolias. They read in the *Times*
how the crickets' chirp has been unchanged for
fifty-five million years. Though such fidelity amuses
her, when she turns to nudge August, it's midnight,
and she's alone. But cricket-song coils and makes
her think of other old things: how the gibbous moon
brings a tidal bulge and small moonquakes, how Venus—
during its night—looks not round but crescent-shaped.

Someone, her friend before August perhaps, has
asked about a lunch date for Monday. Or Thursday.
The days will not hold hands and stay in their circle.
Sunday is no where to be found and has, she believes,
run off with August. The remaining ones, open links, seem
to have become colors instead of placeholders for time.
In the dark, their tones iridesce. She will, she decides
trumpeting a blade of grass, get someone to dial for her,
phone her friend to say they'll meet when it is
yellow and all the old, old, old crickets sing green.

Death Notes In C Minor

1. Dragon Scales

In her path, dragon scales, so she saved pills
and began a trek up a mountain.
As she walked, she rephrased in her head
the note she'd leave behind. Though she wasn't
old, she'd lost or was losing everything.
Now fire-breathing creatures came at night
and stalked her, their C minor chorus
a keening whine as they peeled away bits
of matter. Not what she'd imagined.
Oblivious to dragon scales, she'd dreamed of
an endless sleep in a quilted bed,
a painless drowning, an undisturbed grave.

•

Pocking the mountainside with her stick,
she thought of Mallory on the North Face
of Everest. In a season of scant snow,
something impossibly white, his bare back
gleaming amid still-clinging shreds
of tweed and leather, his skin bleached
the alabaster of a Greek statue. Preserved
by cold for more than seven decades,
each muscle hard and visible. Attached to
an uncoiled length of rope, still reaching up
toward the peak, toward a high grave, he'd left
his messages behind. *This is going to be
more like war than mountaineering.*
Legs broken, arm broken. *I don't expect to
come back.* Goggles and compass in his pocket.
Alone. *Because it's there.*

2. There Yet Not There

Her mountain was, too, and the pills.
But her thoughts skimmed down to sea-level
where someone had found a message
in a bottle. A letter from Private Thomas Hughes
written to his Elizabeth
as he was heading for the Western Front
and found last year by a fisherman
trawling off the Thames Estuary.
1914: twelve days before he died.
Did the message say he loved her?
Did it—in a bottle strong enough to bob
for decades—suggest he was never
coming back? Did he say he was afraid?
Did he say goodbye?

·

As the woman trudged up the mountain,
other posthumous messages obsessed her.
Like Beethoven's lock of hair tested
for DNA, so the world would know
if he'd had syphilis. And Goethe, too,
she pondered, dug up under cover of night,
his body probed, skin stripped off,
dead bones strengthened. Reburied then
without his shroud but with skin replaced
and his laurel wreath glued on. He left
countless messages about death and its meaning
but none more poignant than this: inside
his ruined brain pan—nothing but ash.

·

The mummies, however, found on a icy peak
in Argentina were younger than Goethe and
the woman on the mountain,
yet older, preserved in perfect form for 500 years—
the girl, not damaged or in pain but sacrificed
to Incan gods at the rim of a volcano.
Wasn´t she, the walker, being sacrificed, too?

3. *Danse Macabre*

Her trail was fretted with rock, the angle
steep as she traversed talus and scree, felt
dragon scales slice into feet and head.
Above, the clouds, a filigree of darkness
and light, a frayed slice of rainbow.
She kept seeing Mallory´s whiteness
and a corked bottle afloat for 85 years.
She saw, too, the face of the mummy girl,
organs intact, blood fresh-frozen, saw
Beethoven´s hair and the ashes of Goethe´s
desiccated brain.

        As she picked her way from
rock into snow, the air was thin and cold,
numbing her and her brain. Goethe was dancing

with a mummy in a yellow mantle
and feathered headdress while Beethoven
conducted a C Minor opus about a message
in a bottle, and Mallory, still dragging
a rope from his waist, offered
his canteen and goggles to a soldier
off to the Western Front.
Watching the Dance of Death before her,
struggling for breath and clarity, she
dropped the bottle of pills, knowing
she´d never swallow them. But she let
an army private take her arm, accepted
Goethe´s offer of the old shroud,
took Mallory´s compass. When she heard
the C minor chords, she did not
lie down to sleep in snow but only paused
to mark her journal. *It´s going to be all right,*
she wrote. *I no longer live here. Nor am I*
there. But I have given notice.

Incoherence Of Time

Eddied until the continuum makes no sense:
branches that were bare tremble with leaves.
Dry streambeds run suddenly with water.

The child was by my side. She is under water.
She was in her bed. She is lost in a northern wood.
She was a child of light. She lives now in gloom.

Vases that held masses of rosebuds hold only
stems and a scatter of puckered petals,
and the clear water has a soured yellow cast.

The apartment that was cold is on fire. It is
cinder and ash. The child had socks and shoes.
Now she has chilled feet and nightmares.

An hour vanishes in a breath. A month passes
between tonight's moonrise and moonset.
A bright necklace of hours beads into a year.

This morning, I was taut and lithe as the child.
But tonight my torso and feet are misshapen,
and I am too pain-throbbed to move at all.

Everything here is true. Everything false.
This is the lie of memory. Muscle of memory.
Arrogance of memory. The echo of memory.

The Iron Handle

The Night Mind

There's a broken moon in the lake.
Craters tooth its inner curve,
and the movie has started to reel backwards.
Beach fires flare from coals to flame to log.
Chicken bones arc from the barrel
to the mouth and return firm-fleshed to a plate.
As we dive from iron-red water to springboard,
we're transformed from wet to dry.
Paddling in reverse to the dock, we grow
larger yet younger in every frame.
Atop the totem pole, a girl sits watching
nightwinds eddy pine needles from
the sand and restitch them to the trees.
Because time is ruptured, the girl's hair unbraids
and fingernails shrink. She dreams now
in many tenses. *I am. I was. I used to be...*
Words thin to syllables that fall
like glass beads from the belt she is unweaving,
and they mica the ground below.
Above, the flat cut-out sky presses down
until water fades to black, leaving
only the afterimage of a crazed moon.

Rough And Unsugared

River time was the only time
as we relished the stolen, the borrowed
and the pleasure in each.
Past sandbanks on the Flambeau,
adrenaline high, we whitewatered
in canvas canoes, buoyed by
weightlessness and the edge of risk.
At night, the campfire flared

and, with our counselor, we bellied
down furrows, stole corn to roast.
But, unable to find our tin of salt,
we tucked in shirttails,
hiked to the house by the field
where we—well-mannered thieves—
asked to borrow, even dug in pockets
and offered to pay.

Later, squatting by flames to daunt
mosquito and bear, we charred and ate
the salt-crusted grain, knowing
it was horse-corn—
rough and unsugared. Then we picked
our teeth, smelled both the cobs
and our gamy, high-breasted bodies
dimly aware, as we listened to

fugue of guitar and wave, how theft
and the river had spun us free.

The Iron Handle Of Innisfree

Innisfree: not the bee-wattled glade of Yeats
but Wisconsin by fast-moving water.
Our tents were up. Dinner was squaw-corn
and Ritz apple pie from the campfire oven.
And that night, before the bear came,
my counselor—careful not to touch her body
to mine—leaned toward me under inked pines
and kissed me full on the lips.

Later, after the bear, after morning coffee
with eggshells, we swam the white river across
from Innisfree; and as we—naiads on boulders
ringed by water—lounged, I found the handle,
a heavy iron oval its shaft sunk deep into rock.
Open sesame, I told myself. With a twist,

hidden places might be revealed. As my counselor
eyed me in my two-piece cotton suit,
I took hold of the handle and slipped into the river,
held fast and twisting, tethered yet free.
Then, without looking back, I uncurled my fingers
and let the current fly me downstream
away from rock, iron, flesh: elements that
beggared revelation.

Flight To Primitive Passions

A face that might be her own
materializes amid a nimbus of frantic hair

as she yearns to be in the dust lane
of a spiral galaxy.

Is she all right? Mother asks Sister.

Lulled by the oceanic, a promise
of dissolved boundaries, she seeks

uncoupling—the self
tindered into the cosmos.

You must get the bats, Sister pleads.
They're large and hairy, and Brother is afraid.

Gide froze when ecstasy touched;
yet she courts sublimation,

flight to a rock-strewn plain
with red-sky days.

Our sister the poet isn´t afraid, Brother says, *but knows
nothing of bats. Except for those in her belfry.*

A slide on black ice, a mouse trapped
in webs. First, she must mute voices,

then tame creatures
and exhale herself into the abyss.

She claps to disrupt their sonar, Sister says.
She cradles them in her hands. She sings to them.

A shadow spills on a scrim. Backlit,
shadow becomes sky. Alone in a sky brindled

with cloud and furred wings,
she may not come to rescue again.

Who is she? Mother asks softly. *Do we know her?*

Pantoum For A Member Of The Wedding

It was the summer of fear. A jazz sadness quivered her nerves.
She was an unjoined person. A member of nothing.
The world, she said, *is certainly a sudden place.*
A green sick dream. I wish I was somebody else except me.

She was an unjoined person. A member of nothing.
Too tall for the arbor, she stared into a tangle of vines
A green sick dream. I wish I was somebody else except me.
Remembrances were sudden, each colored by its own season.

Too tall for the arbor, she stared into a tangle of vines
Sun-drunk bluejays screamed and murdered among themselves.
Remembrances were sudden, each colored by its own season.
But in the corner of her eye. Love. A thing not spoken.

Sun-drunk bluejays screamed and murdered among themselves.
The wedding was like a dream outside her power.
But in the corner of her eye. Love. A thing not spoken.
She was a wild girl. Strange words flowered in her throat.

The wedding was like a dream outside her power.
In blue light, she felt as a person drowning.
She was a wild girl. Strange words flowered in her throat.
She heard a chord then, a bell, an unfinished tune.

In blue light, she felt as a person drowning.
It was the summer of fear. A jazz sadness quivered her nerves.
She heard a chord then, a bell, an unfinished tune.
The world, she said, *is certainly a sudden place.*

Blind-Fish Cave

Somewhere on the transparent mountain:
a cave with a shallow lake inside,
and, at night, I come upon it again and again.

Bamboo poles wait there in darkness, propped,
their safety pin hooks unbaited,
yet I lift them, fish with the empty hooks,

catch albino trout to fry over cool fire.
As I chew and swallow, soft flesh-bones
disintegrating between my teeth,

earthworms tunnel beneath me, moles dig
sightlessly, and moonlight leaks through
the trees. Beyond the cave, a world where

birds fly right-side up, and the sun arcs
behind them in the east. There´s a path,
raw and rock-strewn, with miles to traverse

facing prowl of boar and puma. Will I
seek danger? Blistered feet or raked back?
No, I´ll hunker in the cave. Call this

selective hibernation: food, shelter,
exhalation of bat and snake, and echoes
within edgy echoes.

Ice Maiden

Century plants sway, acacias umbrella
the hillsides, and I am cold. Above tufted slopes,
a glacier-slash marks the caldera, and,
beyond, the iced peak of Carambé.
It´s hard to breathe. Not only altitude but fear
of dissolving. Adrenaline pumps
but depletes. Footing is odd because leg-length
is unpredictable and feet deadened.

Above the treeline, tundra where lichen enamels
rock. Babynail flowers—elephant´s head,
moss campion—mat the ground. Bending nauseates.
I move slowly and am left behind. Children
pass me. A sun-brown girl with fishing pole
who might be my body-double
smiles and, in English, confides, *Next time
I do this, I´m going to bring a horse.*

One by one I shed pack, stick, history, as I
slog through snowmelt on the last switchback.
My feet slalom, but then I see a blue skin
of water burning the surface of an alpine lake.
No one is here. Not the girl-child.
Not my companions. Only peaks of granite
and snow refracting sunlight.
Cloud-shadows finger me, frost my cheeks.

In the lake, icebergs and an image of my face.
Thin air. Thin sun. Thin ice.
I hold my breath. The water in this lake
is so cold, I may be preserved forever.

Deathscapes

Richmond Heights, Missouri, 1947

Rosemarie was skinny, ugly, and mean.
She cheated at Monopoly and tattled.
Once at our house she peed the bed
on purpose, and once she stole trading cards.
Even if she was two years older,
she wasn´t as smart as I was, couldn´t skate
as well or run as fast. When I told
our neighbor Mrs. Knabe how much I hated
Rosemarie and why, Mrs. Knabe said,
You must be nice to her, because she has
leukemia and is going to die.

Winter, Wisconsin, 1953

We were summer camp girls trying on clothes,
slumming, laughing at ruffles and peplums,
cheap, shiny fabrics. Then a woman
with clogs and a kerchief stepped inside
the dress shop. As I frowned at plaid
dotted Swiss, eyed her sun-leathered face
reflected to forever in the three-way mirror,
she told the salesgirl how her husband
had slunk to the henhouse the night before
and shot himself in the head. *All morning,*
she said, *I was mopping up his brains*
and trying to calm the chickens.

Detroit, Michigan, 1962

Anne was a teenager, only 15 when her father
fell to the ground, mouth foaming,
incoherent noise ratcheting from his throat,
and she—a large, sedentary girl—vaulted
a hedge to get to him, dropped to her knees,
gave mouth-to-mouth respiration while
her mother ran across the street crying for help.
I'd never kissed a man on the lips,
she confided, *and there I was tasting*
my father's saliva, giving him his last kiss.

Ladue, Missouri, 1970

Aunt Eleanor was beautiful—tiny and dark.
She wore silk, cashmere, diamond earrings,
had a doctor ex-husband who was
impotent and hated her, an adopted daughter
who didn't much like her either,
and each month she borrowed money
from her brother-in-law, my father.
One day Bee, her old nursemaid, found her
hanging by the neck wearing a kimono
and one diamond stud. Suicide, the family
agreed, and never mentioned her again.
But Bee said, *Rope too high, stepladder*
too low, and I knows it was
Dr. Joe put her there and stole that jewel.

San Francisco, California, 1973

Lying in the hospital bed, a man I loved.
The only sound: slosh of dialysis,
as his blood washed while we held hands.
When a wave of dementia blurred
his brain, he clawed at me, whined like
a child for me to hold the urinal. Instead, I
called his wife. Later, he and I, holding hands
again, knowing this was the last night,
an overdose of morphine to follow, said
our good-byes. When I leaned down, he
kissed my lips, murmuring, *Strawberries...*
you taste like strawberries.

St. Louis, Missouri, 1978

My father, dying of cancer, throat ulcerated
from chemotherapy, told me
if hospital windows weren´t fused shut,
he´d jump, if he had his squirrel gun
he´d shoot himself, had rat poison
from the basement he´d swallow it
in his protein shake. He wanted only me,
he said, because my mother couldn´t admit
he was dying, so he had to pretend.
Only I understood and put him at ease.
So I packed my suitcase and left.
Five days later, addressing his last words
to my mother, he died. *Your price is far above*
rubies, he told her, quoting from Proverbs.
You are a woman of valor.

Rome, Italy, 1986

A young artist, lay down for a nap. She´d been
depressed, slept a lot, so her roommates
didn´t wake her. But later, after dinner
and the movies, they found her
poisoned by gas from a faulty heater.
At a posthumous exhibit
of her photo-collages, I stared into
her black-gray-white, unsuspecting face;
and two years later, her father, a dispassionate
lawyer, told me, *It´s all ashes, you know.*
Losing a child ruins your life.

Cambridge, Massachussets, 1992

Walking through a graveyard where I have
no attachment except to the long-dead
like Bullfinch or Julia Ward Howe,
talking not of death but of dogwood blooming,
and names from headstones a son might use
for his new baby. Caleb? Jonah?
Hebrew names, because those New Englanders
were Hebrew scholars who lived when death
was contagious as many still believe it is.
Disembodied breath shivers headstones as we
move by, making me wonder what I will say.
Where and to whom when incantations fail
to protect, when shadows no longer couple,
when rags of dreams shred in the light
as I whisper, *Yes...* Or, *No...* Or nothing.

The Book Of Responses

Conversa el humo con las nubes?

–Pablo Neruda, **The Book Of Questions**

You Don't Believe That Dromedaries Keep Moonlight In Their Humps?

Petra

As flower moon kindles the cliffs and valleys,
the river's a snake with pearled scales.
For the man and woman: a camel ride
through the sikh, their cheeks and bodies roughed
by coats of silt. Petra city of sandstone,
shifts in a rosy wind. The lovers find
ancient rings, a Bedouin teapot, each other.
Then exchanging rings, they set
the mesa with shards and brew thick, sweet tea.

Where the camel is tethered there is no water.
He whickers, but the two can hear only one another,
so while they sigh, pick bright poppies
to weave in the woman's darkest hair,
the camel opens his mouth to drink in moonlight.

Arouane

In Arouane, six camel-days from Timbuktu,
the travelers see Sandwoman.
From the blackness of the village master's house,
she trudges into light bearing bowls of sand.
Her work, a lifetime's work:
keep sand from choking the oasis.

eclipse in dark and simple silence, earth-curved umbra
skeins the moon with slippery ease a last sly smile shines

At sunset, Sandwoman slumps on her doorstep,
grit in body crevices and in the rice
finger-scooped from her bowl,
and she sees the night-camel swallow the moon.
Because the beast is stealing something,
she flings her bowl at his head.

moon-blushes cratered mares deepen, mountains spike
date, orange, honey hoop of color solemn face of night

As the bowl drops, a silvered moon-edge appears.
Sandwoman staggers up, dances, because she—
old as she is—has made
the night-camel spit out the moon.
Still, that evil bag of bones is a thief
who has inhaled some of the moon's fire.

Luxor

Night market in Luxor under a pregnant moon
as the travelers, forbidden lovers, walk past stalls
flush with sunrise vegetables and fruit.

She tells him of another Nile adventure in another life:
an oasis, a tent, and how caravans of ghost camels
arched and stalked through midnight skies.

He calls her sloe-eyed Cleopatra, says all poets lie.
Then the two lace fingertips and wander
past saffron and cinnamon and vials of aphrodisiac.

They find peacock djellabahs scrolled with silk,
trade beads on golden thread, tethered goats
and churring birds. But as they admire creamy feathers,

a boy beheads a pair of pigeons, then knifes
the throat of a bleating kid. Blood pulses,
stains them both, and she—sure this is an omen—

flees, heading west to sand and sky, until, uncoupled,
she sees at her feet puzzled bones and overhead
a camel-shaped cloud, its hump sluiced with moonlight.

An Unmeasured Life

Would It Be Best To Outlaw
Interplanetary Kisses?

To find him, she didn´t orbit
the dark side of Venus. He was there
idling across the street in front of her bike.
Slim, tanned, his walk
something between a prance and a dawdle.
A shivered whine to his voice.

As she watched, he arched from the outline of
his body, static yet moving—a Duchamps painting
of the displaced.

Tarred roadbed graveled through
a tissue of faded jeans and leather jacket.
His face dismissed lips
and teeth and tongue.
Wholeness became separation, levitating

a disjointed sorcerer. The air was dense
with fragments. She was afraid
to steer around or through him.
His lips floated free,

tongue sought her ear, loose fingers
seized handlebars. Desperate, she furled her lashes
and leaned forward until chain-song
blotted out his whispers,
his dangerous alien interplanetary kisses.

What Is The Distance In Round Meters
Between The Sun And The Oranges?

She dreamed herself
into the Dickinson house
and put on Emily´s clothes.
Shrouded in white cotton,
she meant to haunt Amherst,
inhaling time.
She wanted a soft song of restraint,
path of easy pain,
season without sun or oranges,

a sudden winter where
she could boot across cobblestone,
pause by a pond and watch
fish shadows in the shallows beneath ice.
Mindfulness rather than
unsifted chaos.

In a January thaw, she´d remember
how maidenhair uncurls in April
and hummingbird sips
nectar of a wild white azalea.
As Emily, she could spend
half-lit winter days
baking black cake
while she guessed how to reckon
distance or a life in round meters.

How Did The Abandoned Bicycle
Win Its Freedom?

Her bicycle brought her there.
Throwing it down, she waded
into the pool, watching the angled
flippers of young sea turtles,
circling and circling.

Their shells: scallops of orange
and blue overlaid with algae.
Together and apart, past a weir gate,
they swam recycled sea water,
rippled on to nowhere.

Turtle dreams and hers, too: open sea,
wave and cloud and azure purpling past the reef.
Full moon nights and urgent coupling.

When summer comes and gates lift,
turtles will know free peril
in the sea. Yet, when summer comes,
she will still be indolent in a small pool
eyeing the ocean near by.

For her, no release but more circles
within circles. She'll remain
in the shallows. And, if she rises
from the pool, looks back,
even the old bicycle may be gone.

If The Butterfly Transmogrifies
Does It Turn Into A Flying Fish?

Moorish idols pair mouth to mouth,
dorsal fins flick like antennae:
two yellow-black wings,
a silent flutter in coral.

Fish or butterfly? she asks herself,
the arc of brightness a tease.
As in an Escher print—perception.
To poise over or under the wave´s lip,

know wide-eyed flight into
precariousness. For the butterfly,
a single season. For fish,
danger but long liquid years.

Butterfly aches to be fish in flight,
the thrill of drowning
in air. Risk without promise.
Soar before plunge.

Not transmogrified but suspended.
A rare dream.
Tempted by time and by
the freedom of gaudy moments.

For The Diseased What Color Do You Think April Is?

She was remembering the April of violets.
April of redwings in a cattail marsh,
of crinkled daffodil throats.
April of fields tipped green,
of gray lambs flocked on a hillside,
of mud-twitch minnows in a pond.

Now she knows snow on thorned vines,
the ice of snow-burn.
She's rootbound,
so it's hard to think or move—
inward-pointing thorns sharper and sharper,

lacerating, until she begins to see
only the white-black, black-white shades
of a sudden blackberry winter.

And What Was Beating In The Night?
Were They Planets Or Horseshoes?

As she lies wrapped in winter down,
she hears ghost horses gallop
the night sky. Then she sees them
with their comet tails
and manes of the Milky Way.

Come, they urge, touching her cheeks with
their velvety tongues. *We'll take you along.*

As she prays for silence,
the hoofbeats grow louder.
Other galaxies, new songs, they promise,
green cheese left behind
when the cow jumped the moon,
or white rivers where she might drink
and be drunk with joy.

*Faster than you can run, farther than
you have dreamed—a ride out of time.*

Her alien planet of a heart picks up
the beat, urging *yes* and *now,*
dismissing *why* and *maybe* and *what if,*
as it tries to break free of gravity,
and open its cool white cage of bone.

And Do You Know Which Is Harder,
To Let Run To Seed Or To Do The Picking?

The turtles are gone, but the bicycle is
back. Neither oranges nor sun
has ever been measured. The pond has
trout and monarchs but no flying fish.
Night-stallions have fled
to another galaxy with her heart.

No more interplanetary kisses, therefore
no more interplanetary lies. She´s learned
to ignore the thorns and live with laceration.

Hitching up her long white dress, she rides
the rusted bicycle from winter into
blackberry summer where she kneels
heedlessly, picks and picks,
ignoring the berries that will run to seed,
as she fills her mouth with solemn fruit.

Am I Allowed To Ask My Book
Whether It's True I Wrote it?

It must have been someone else,
someone out-of-control.
This volume is elusive as carp
in a pond. I dip into it,
but past the shiny surface,
purple restlessness and broken borders,
always the dark surprise.
Secrets held close, like those
folded in pleats of a Japanese fan—

waterfall, bridge, forbidden tryst.
Or in petroglyphs. Does that one mean
sun or drought? Does the one below
mean cloud or storm?
And the lovers notched in stone,
are they moving together or apart?
Book, fan, petroglyph: each one
an old mystery to decode.

Carp skim with such idle beauty.
For an instant I see through
their fish eyes, but later
what I knew is only an echo of an echo.
Who was I at twenty? At forty?
Who wrote these words?
If we were reintroduced,
would I be face-to-face with
a friend or an unmeasured stranger?

Where Do The Things In Dreams Go?
Do They Pass To The Dreams Of Others?

Wakeful Rest

Sleep—a house barred by a moat,
house with a gate I can´t pass through
or one where the door will not open.

I am prey, and a midnight cat is toying with me,
or I´m manzanita choked by periwinkle.
I feel outlined in black, yet the pages
of my books are blank, because their ink
has leaked away and pooled into darkness.

Lying there, my hair and nails grow
as they will after death, and I fear
my shadow will chase me toward chaos
vivid as Larium dreams. To stay alert,
I begin to pluck mushrooms from the air:
candy caps, witches´ butter, hen-of-the-woods,

but I find myself swimming toward them,
angling submerged forests like a reef fish.
Fish, I know, never sleep.
Instead, like all the cold-blooded, they sink
into wakeful rest. So, floating face-down, tasting
witches´ butter, yielding my cold-blooded self,
liquid spine and mosaic of lapped scales,
I undulate toward this suspended state.

Starcatchers

As the Pleiades rise and set, we are floating
on the corrugated lake,
feeling the sway of a forest of kelp
and curious, darting mouths of minnows.

Our mouths, too, are curious and our fingers.
They probe, touching one another,
ourselves as our dreams intertwine.
Suspended here, our faces and bodies are

no longer exhausted by the effort of
growing old. Now, lithe and buoyant
again, we ignore the shiver of bat wings,
sound of nightmares riding the wind.

Above us, a fishtail sky with a black moon,
and our full-fleshed selves hide behind it
while their hinged shadows rise
and begin to reach for falling stars.

Dark Matter

Glass dreams—the Chihuly nebula,
bowls within bowls within bowls, infinity
on a table top; and in the distant universe,

a billion years before stars blinked light:
exotic particles, black holes so dense
nothing escapes. We peer into the bowls,

try to recapture the dark matter of dreams,

things that shone cold and canny before morning
and burst like the cores of ancient galaxies,
strewing fragments into parallel space.

Is The Sun The Same As Yesterday's
Or Is This Fire Different From That Fire?

Marmaris

Morning sun chokes off the night-dark
as water sparks against the hull
and turquoise streaks ahead

speaking of who I am or might be
until I'm staring into a crazed mirror
of the self

and of you. This is an inscape
with odd illumination and perception
of deeper patterns.

How long, then, have we waited

for the unity of sudden moments,
hunch of dolphin and wake of sailfish,
wedged between

separation and solitude?
Morning radiance strews messages
of promise

shadowed by dream leakage of night.
Though I drink it in,
I cannot quench my thirst.

Caunos

At noon, as heat assaults us and a fig tree
twitches branch and leaf from a fissure of rock,

I sit in the agora trying
to decipher you and broken stones of the past.

Upriver, the necropolis whispers
that the last vanity of the dying is vanity,

that root and water are ardent enough to
split marble. Aware this fire will shudder

into the cold of night, we tongue ripe figs
and let champagne grapes burst upon the palate.

But still, though flesh of fig
and purple-black grape sweetens

your terror and mine, I cannot tell
the ancient stones any more than I can tell you.

Gorëme

In the tufa, ancient homes and shrines
slough Ionic columns and facades.
Yesterday´s rock—today´s sand,
the terror of impermanence.

Again and again, a Byzantine St. George
who looks like you
slays a dragon that resembles
a coiled snake.

Over centuries, frescoes recede
until even indigo flakes and veils.
St. George, astride his horse, is leaving,
and I can´t bring him or anything back.

Where rock is split, a landslide
keeps its violent promise,
a mad tumble
until nothing remains

but the fading dragon slayer
and fiery dust—
a permanent impermanence.

Antalya

You never worry that I am at sea
as mist scrims islands and mountains
into a puzzle of swell and sky and fir
where mysteries fuse
the half-assembled pieces.

Soft-needled pines, rootbound to the cliffs,
are unmoved by mortality.
But my fear is fragmented from today
into the depths of tomorrow; and because
you never worry about light, I do.

All happiness, my love, is temporary madness
with the dark embedded.

You are a magician who draws doves
and sabers and words, but do you
have spells to cure sun blindness caused by
the shook fire of open sea? Can you change
tomorrow? Can you save the light?

A dove on a pine branch flutes a tune
redolent with passion and sadness,
his dropped feather, gray-white,
the only quill to tell of shadowed romance.
If you were here, I´d offer the feather

and make you worry me through darkness
into a hemisphere of light.

Does He Know That I Never Loved Him And That He Never Loved Me?

Singita: Artful Matter

What she loved was who she was
when she was with him.
What he loved was the game,
himself pursuing her. For them,
a serpentless Eden in a sealed globe
where palm and sand and water,
turtle and butterfly,
intermingle when inverted.

All that matters, he said, as he cradled the globe
till it opened by itself and a river flowed out
with whitecaps curled and pulsing
like those in a Hokusai print, *is artful matter.*

But the river could not be recalled.
Turtle was more than a shell,
butterfly more than a wing,
fruit was less than the tree,
and the globe had a price tag on it.
Sometimes when logic is lost,
agitation makes summer sand sting
like white-barbed flakes of snow.

M´boma: Tidal Shift

Loose cuff of summer, tremor of morning,
and she tasted, he said, like starfish and honey.

Slow-motion time, her pulse tamped
as if she were submerged, as heartbeats of

all mammals slow when they dive,
a phenomenon from primordial waters.

This will never happen again, she tells herself,
stunned by the shift of desert tides.

Though her landscape was once swell of ocean,
she rocks now in the wake of a drying sea.

Xudum: Hallucination

The man and woman are dark and light,
imperfect and moon-mad.
The light and dark faces of the moon
have different values, too,
yet all are cold under the Southern Cross.

The mares are dry and barren,
mountains sharp, and the lovers
can explore only at night.
Together, they may see the moon rise,
but they'll never see it set.

He, with his short span of attention,
will look away first. While the round O
of the moon-mouth freezes her eye,
he'll wander off, eager
to explore thawed shades of morning.

Soon, he'll hallucinate this tale from his pen,
tattoo a wild white azalea
on her untouched breast,
putting her astride a moon-drunk camel
and disguising her
with a hot cascade of blood-red hair.

Do You Not Also Sense Danger
In The Sea's Laughter?

Three ravens strut on the sand,
pecking eyes and liver
of a dead gull.

They claim the scarred table,
wild to devour
the last crumbs of the feast.

Lured by aubergine medley
of well-oiled feather,
I lunge toward them,

but where they were,
no barbed souvenir or down,
only dark laughter

as three ravens preen on a branch
of twisted cedar,
beady and without remorse.

Who Can Convince The Sea To Be Reasonable?

Let the landscape be white and flat far as the eye can see.
Let the seas be ink agitated by unseen monsters
and the golden fish expelled to gasp yet dazzle on the shore.
Let the wings overhead be long-feathered,
while all the black and white and burnished creatures
of sea and land and sky
whisper their songs, unlock the Babel of their tongues,
offer up steps to the sun dance, ghost dance, the dance for
fishes and loaves and manna, for radiant poppies and tulips.
Let the albatross make their nests on the sand
and the golden fish walk together from the margin
with new knowledge of the meaning of light and air.

Notes

Page 6   The quotes used in this poem are from **Cassatt & Her Circle: Selected Letters,** Nancy Mowell Mathews (Abbeville Press, Inc).

Page 9   "zero at the bone" is a phrase Emily Dickinson used in a poem written in 1865. Its first line is: "A narrow fellow in the grass."

Page 25   "Mischling" is a German word meaning "half-breed."

Page 28   This poem is about Karla Faye Tucker, who was executed in Houston, Texas in 1998. She was the first female inmate executed in the U.S. since the Civil War.

Page 46   The lines quoted in this poem come from **A Member of the Wedding** by Carson McCullers (Bantam Books).

The questions used as titles and subtitles in the last section of this book, The Book of Responses, come from The Book of Questions by Pablo Neruda, translated by William O'Daly (Copper Canyon Press). The Book of Responses:

Page 55   *Conversa el humo con las nubes?* (Does smoke talk with the clouds?), poem IV.

Page 57   You Don't Believe That Dromedaries / Keep Moonlight In Their Humps?, poem LVI.

Page 60   Would It Be Best To Outlaw / Interplanetary Kisses?, poem XXIX.

Page 61   What Is The Distance In Round Meters / Between The Sun And The Oranges?, poem XXIX.

Page 62   How Did The Abandoned Bicycle / Win Its Freedom?, poem XV.

Page 63   If The Butterfly Transmogrifies / Does It Turn Into A Flying Fish?, poem XXIII.

Page 64   For The Diseased What Color / Do You Think April Is?, poem XVIII.

Page 65   And What Was Beating In The Night / Were They Planets Or Horseshoes?, poem LVIII.

Page 66   And Do You Know Which Is Harder / To Let Run To Seed Or To Do The Picking?, poem XVIII.

Page 67   Am I Allowed To Ask My Book / Whether It's True I Wrote It?, poem XXI.

Page 68   Where Do The Things In Dreams Go? / Do They Pass To The Dreams Of Others?, poem XLIII.

Page 71   Is The Sun The Same As Yesterday's / Or Is The Fire Different From That Fire?, poem IX.

Page 75   Does He Know I Never Loved Him / And That He Never Loved Me?, poem XLIV.

Page 78   Do You Not Also Sense Danger / In The Sea's Laughter?, poem XXXIX.

Page 79   Who Can Convince The Sea To Be Reasonable?, poem L.

Susan Terris

Susan Terris has had poetry published in many journals including *The Antioch Review, The Midwest Quarterly, Ploughshares, Calyx, Shenandoah, Hunger Mountain, Hotel Amerika, Missouri Review, The Sun,* and *Southern California Anthology.* NATURAL DEFENSES is her first book with Marsh Hawk Press. Other recent books are: POETIC LICENSE (Adastra, 2004), FIRE IS FAVORABLE TO THE DREAMER (Arctos Press, 2003), CURVED SPACE (La Jolla Poets Press, 1998), EYE OF THE HOLOCAUST (Arctos Press, 1999) and ANGELS OF BATAAN (Pudding House Publications, 1999). Recent fiction: NELL'S QUILT (Farrar, Straus & Giroux). In the last four years Ms. Terris has had 12 different poems nominated for Pushcart Awards. She has won many prizes for her work, including the 2003 George Bogin Award offered by the Poetry Society of America.

With CB Follett, she is co-editor of an annual anthology, *RUNES, A Review Of Poetry.* She and her husband David live in San Francisco.

With special thanks to CB ('Lyn) Follett, David St. John, and Sharon Dolin for their enthusiasm, encouragement, and editorial advice.